BOOK FOUR
A DOZEN A DAY

T0024991

Technical Exercises
FOR THE PIANO
to be done each day
BEFORE *practicing*

by

Edna Mae Burnam

Includes Online Audio Orchestrations by Ric Ianonne

PLAYBACK+
Speed • Pitch • Balance • Loop

The exclusive **PLAYBACK+** feature allows tempo changes without altering the pitch.
Loop points can also be set for repetition of tricky measures.

To access audio, visit:
www.halleonard.com/mylibrary

1828-4332-2107-0656

ISBN 978-1-4234-5293-5

WILLIS MUSIC

EXCLUSIVELY DISTRIBUTED BY

HAL•LEONARD®

7777 W. BLUEMOUND RD. P.O. BOX 13819
MILWAUKEE, WISCONSIN 53213

Visit Hal Leonard Online at
www.halleonard.com

A DOZEN A DAY

Many people do exercises every morning before they go to work.

Likewise, we should give our fingers exercises every day *before* we begin our practicing.

The purpose of this book is to help develop strong hands and flexible fingers.

The finger exercises may be played slowly and softly at first, then gradually faster and louder.

The chord exercises may be played *mp*, *mf*, and *f* for variation, and at a moderate rate of speed.

Do not try to learn the entire first dozen exercises the first week you study this book! Just learn two or three exercises, and do them each day *before* practicing. When these are mastered, add another, then another, and keep adding until the 12 can be played perfectly.

When the first dozen – or Group I – has been mastered and perfected, Group II may be introduced in the same manner, and so on for the other Groups.

Many of these exercises may be transposed to different keys. In fact, this should be encouraged.

EDNA MAE BURNAM

INDEX

Group I

1. Running Upstairs And Downstairs

Repeat 3 times before playing ending.
Play swiftly - accenting on key note.

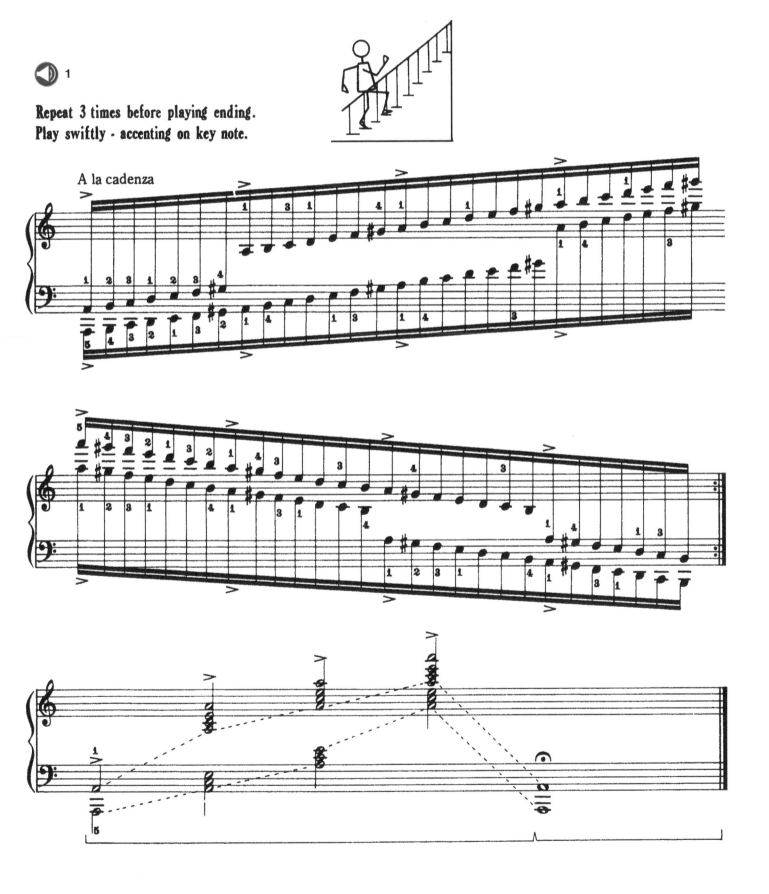

4

2. Sprinting

🔊 2

Repeat 5 times before playing ending.

3. Flinging Arms

🔊 3

Repeat 5 times before playing ending.

4. Daddy Long Leg Steps

🔊 4

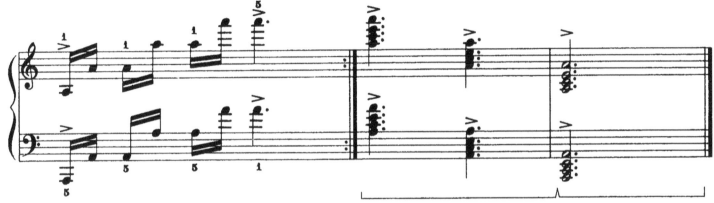

5. Punching Bag

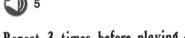 5

Repeat 3 times before playing ending.

6. Deep Breathing

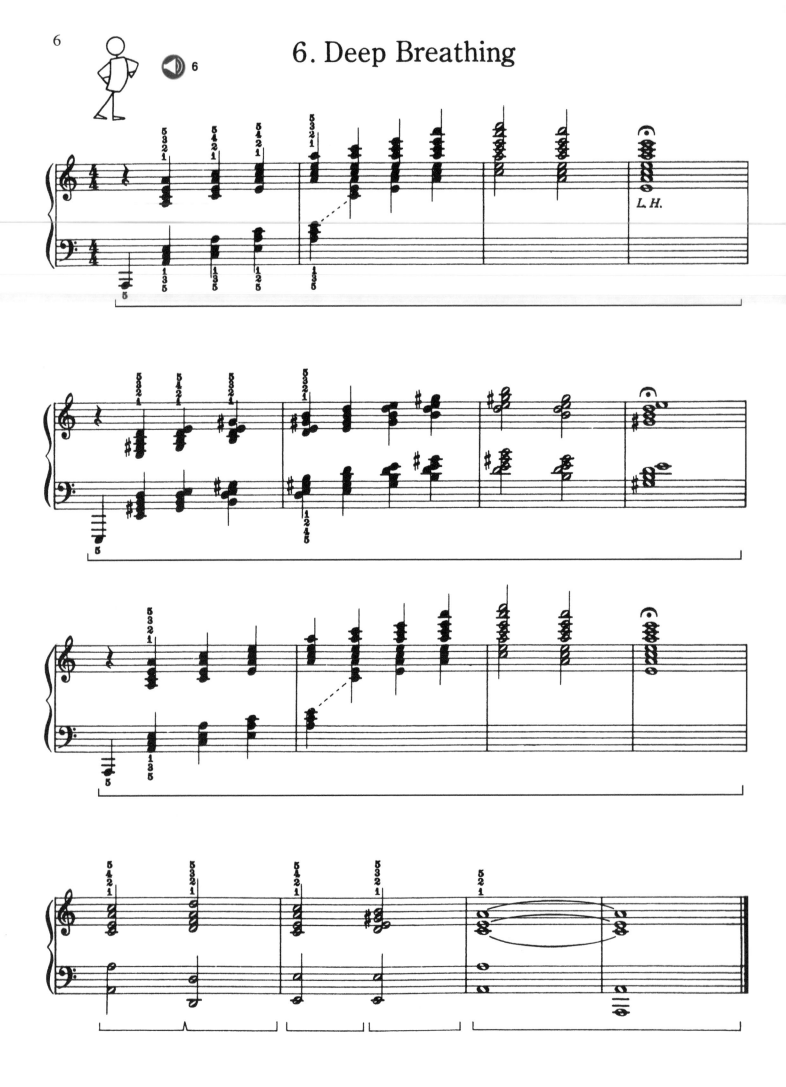

7. Climbing Up And Down A Ladder Fast

8. Jumping

9. Elbow Flip

10. Cross Legged Kick

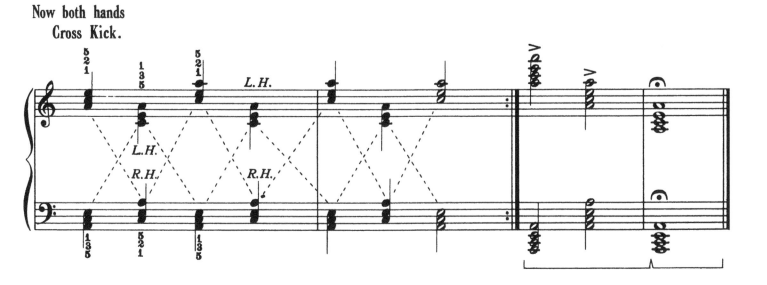

Right hand only!

Left hand alone

Now both hands
Cross Kick.

11. Push Ups

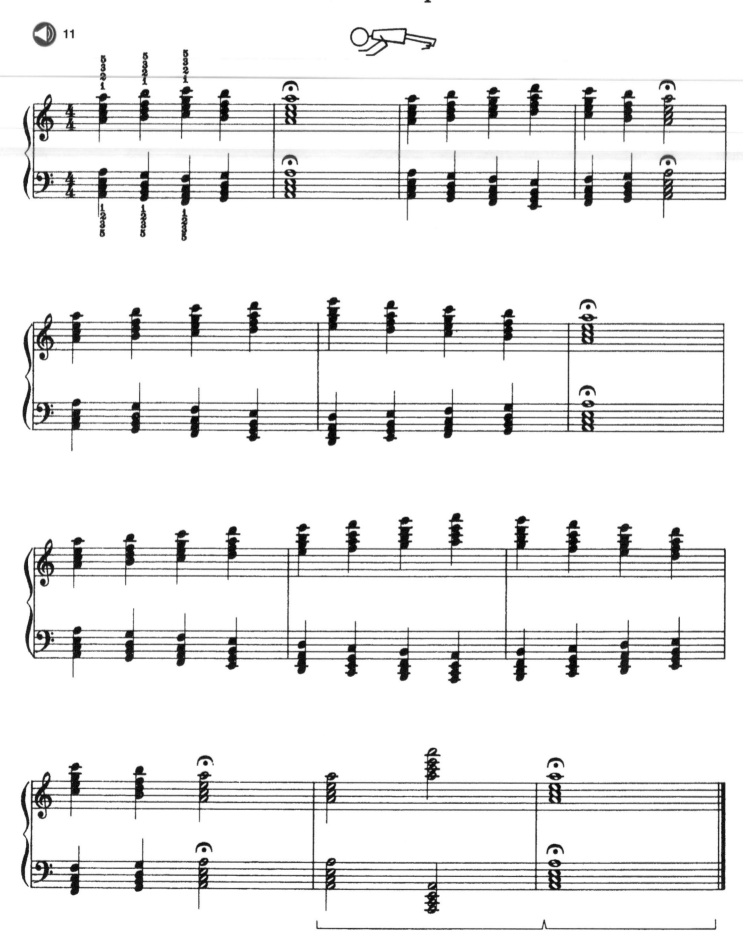

12. Fit As A Fiddle And Ready To Go!

Group II

Four kinds of triads (in chord or arpeggio form)

1. Major ·······································Sign for major   +
2. Minor ·······································Sign for minor   −
3. Diminished ····························Sign for diminished   ○
4. Augmented ····························Sign for   augmented   ++

Here is a
Major triad···>

To change a major triad
to a minor triad lower
the third one half step ·······················>

To change a major triad
a diminished triad lower the
third and fifth one half step ·············>

To change a major triad to
an augmented triad raise
the fifth one half step ·······················>
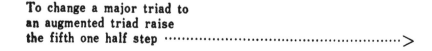

1. Cartwheels

2. The Splits

3. Stretching Right Leg Up

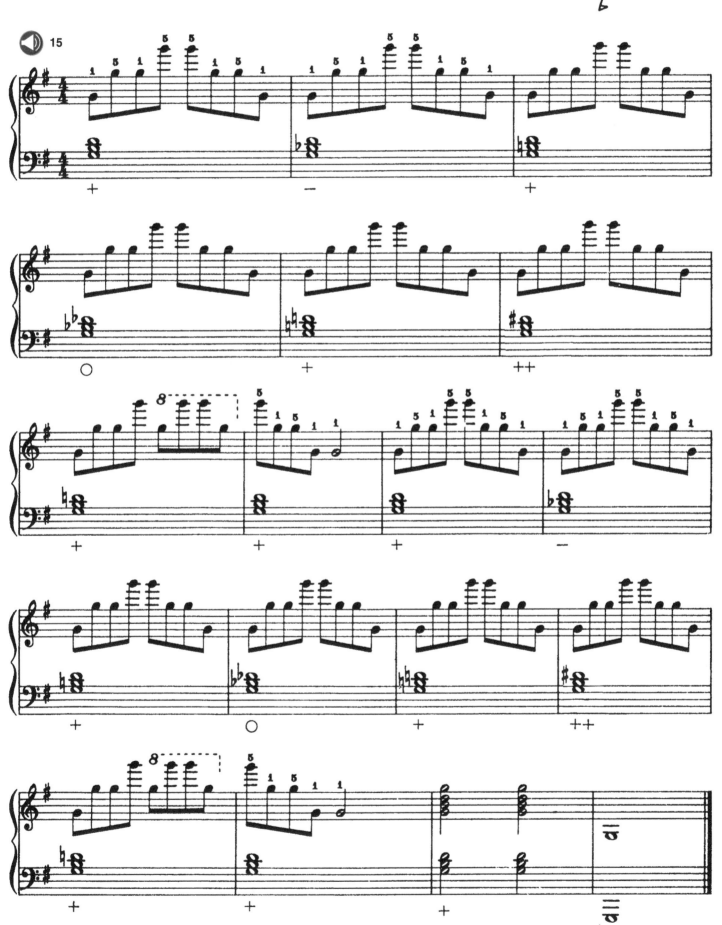

4. Kicking Left Leg Up

5. Boxing

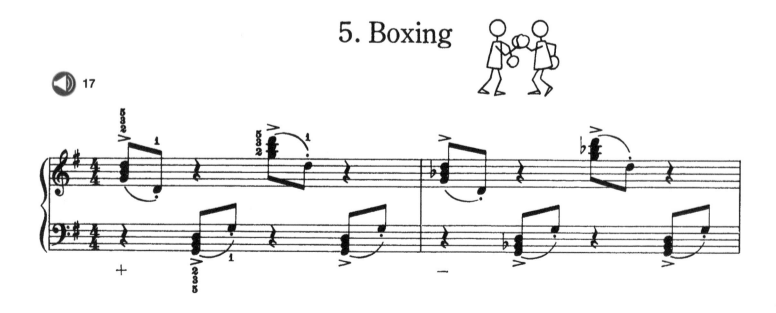

18

6. Windmill Arms

7. Jumping

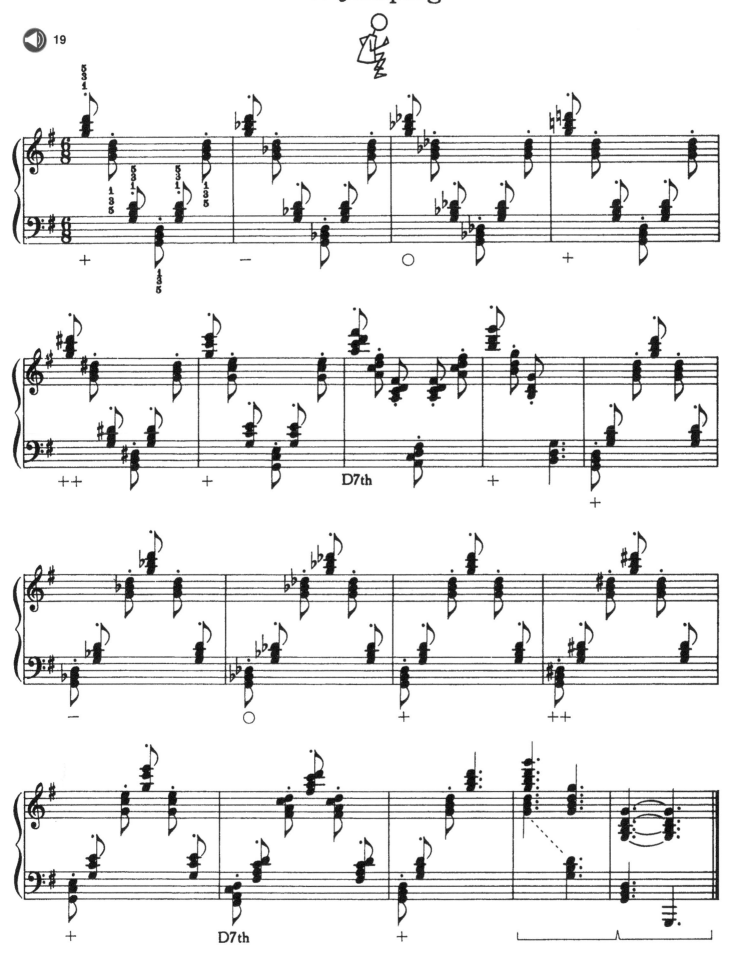

8. Skipping

9. Practicing Golf Drive

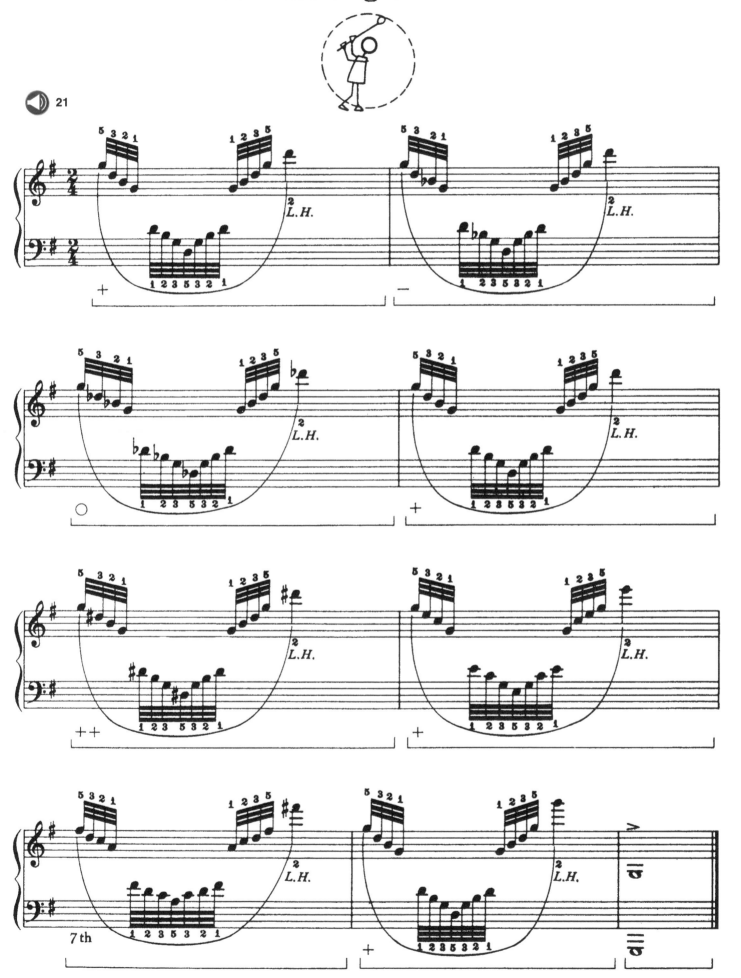

10. Pole Vaulting

11. Deep Breathing

24

12. Fit As A Fiddle And Ready To Go!

Group III

1. Cartwheels

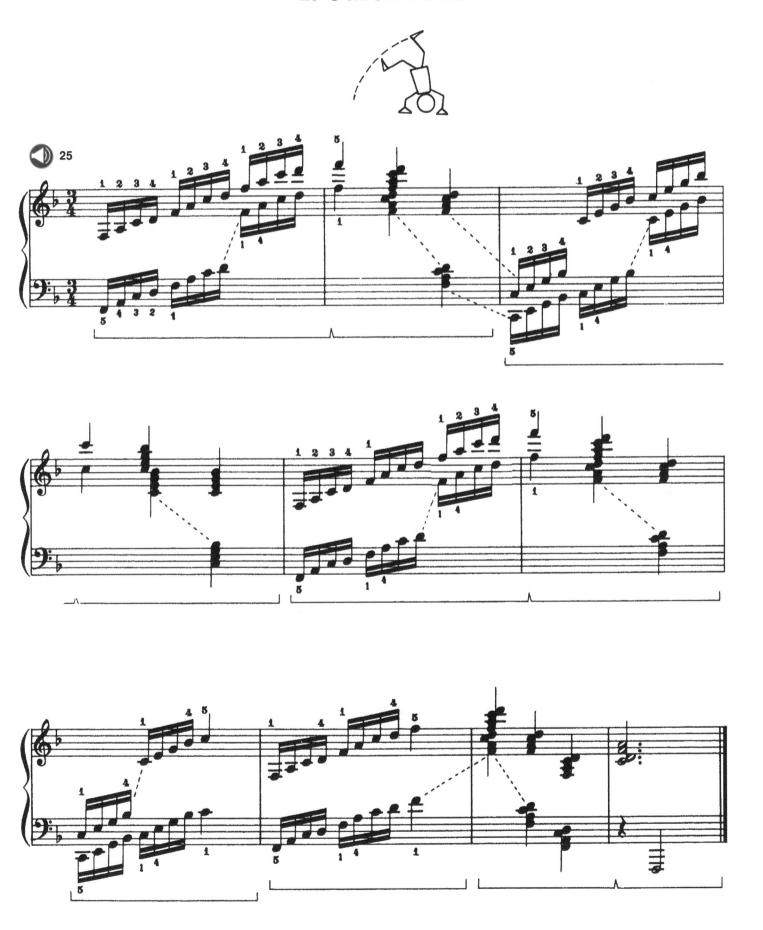

2. The Splits

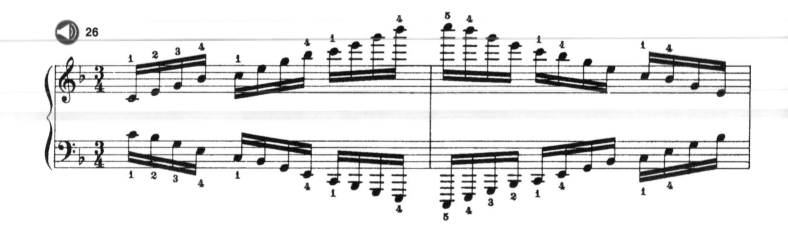

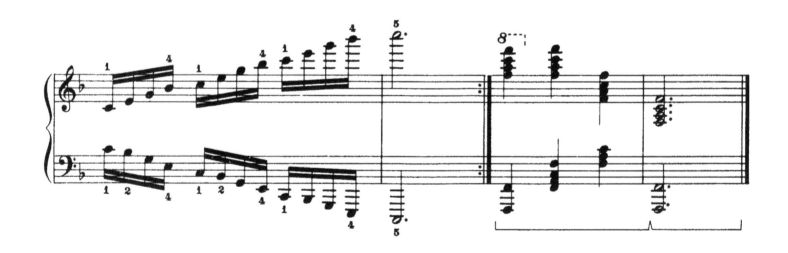

3. Leap Frog

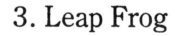

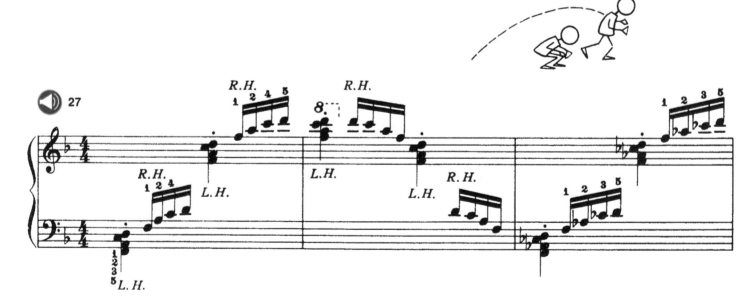

28

4. Juggling Tenpins

5. Golf Practice

A la cadenza

L. H.

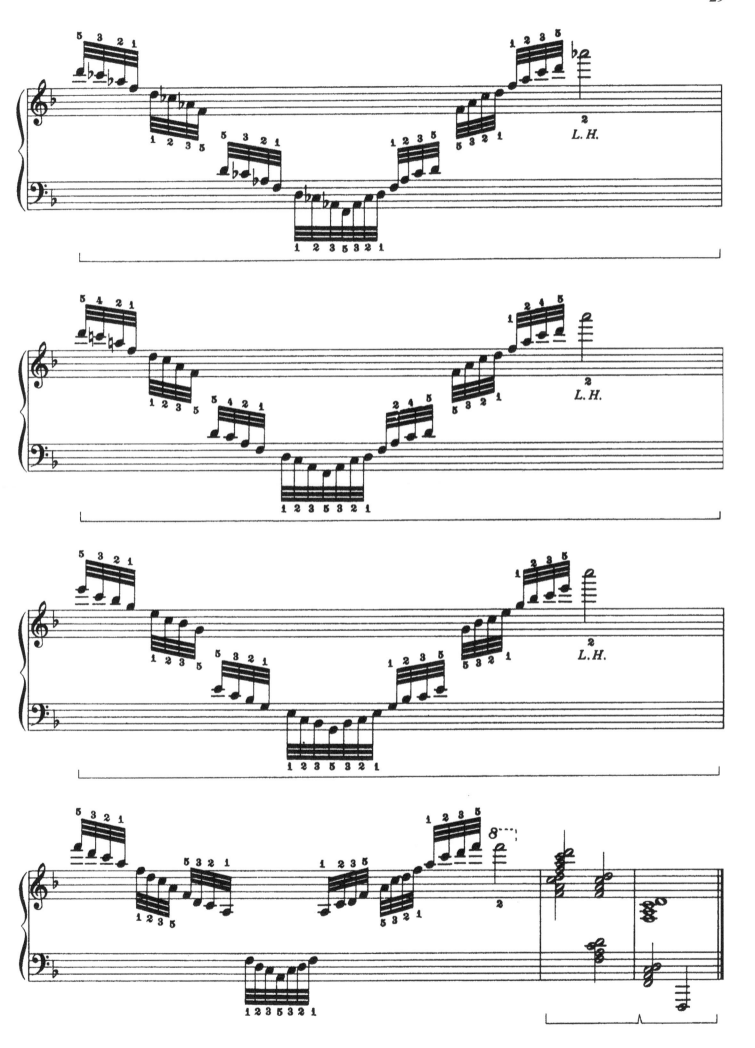

6. Flinging Arms Out And Jumping

7. Deep Breathing

8. Playing Tennis

9. Follow The Leader

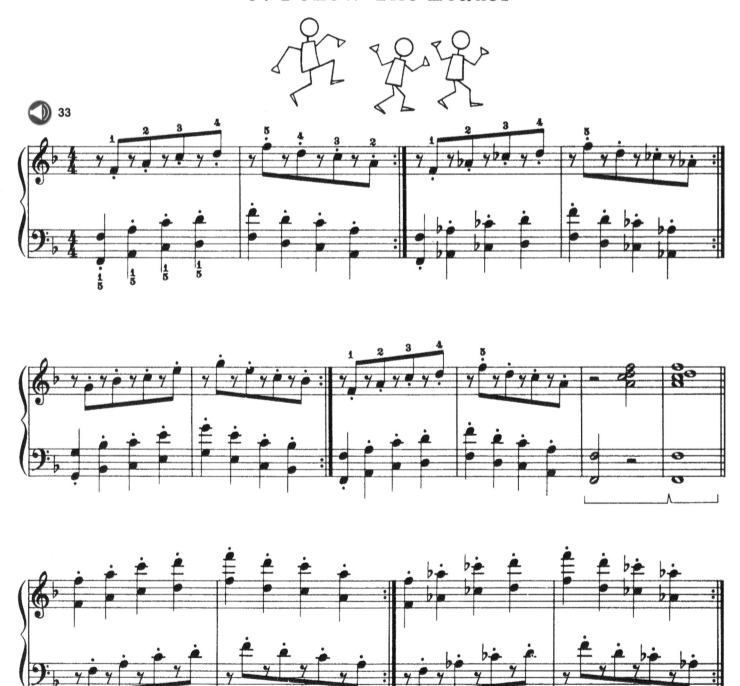

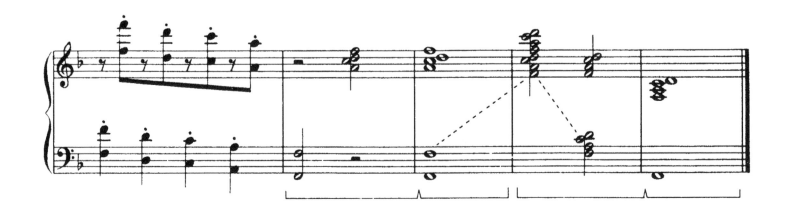

10. Spider Walk

11. Climbing Up And Down A Ladder Fast

12. Fit As A Fiddle And Ready To Go

Group IV

1. Twirls On Toes

2. Riding A Surf Board

3. Flutter Kick While Sitting On A Chair

4. Swinging Leg Like A Pendulum

5. Jump Rope

41

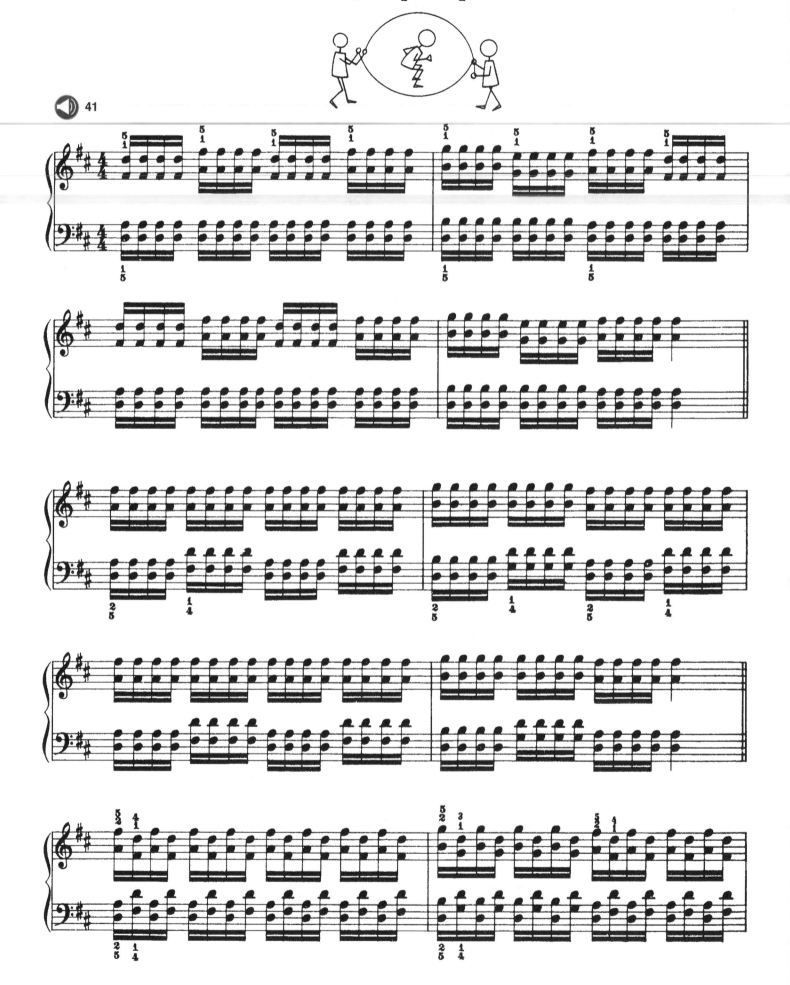

6. Tip Toe Running (In Place)

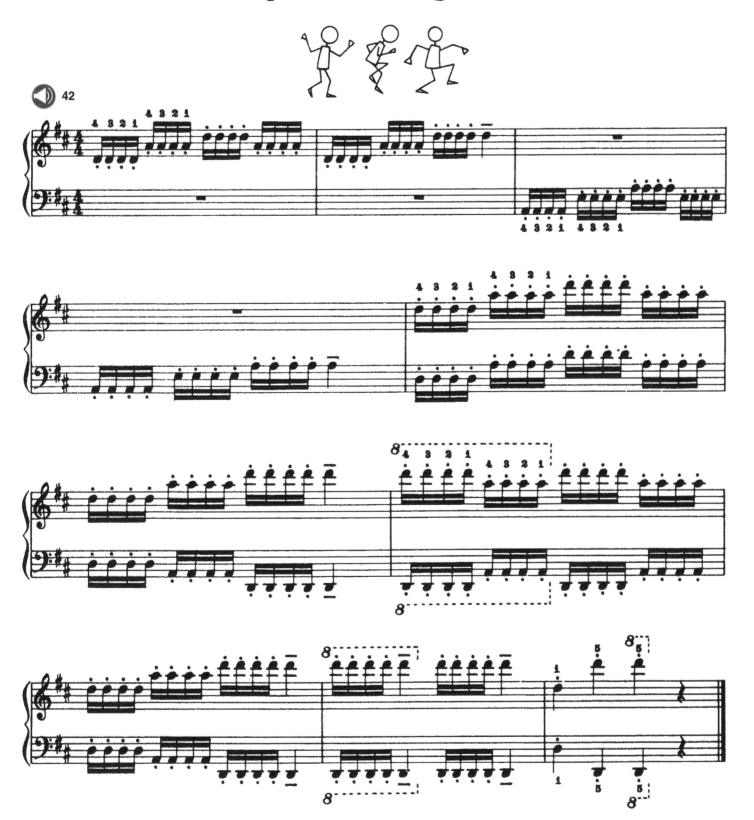

44

7. Jumping On Tip Toe (Like A Kitten)

Alternate hands
Stems up · RH
Stems down · LH

8. Drum Majorette Practice

9. Fast Running

10. Spider Walk

11. Pulley Weight Pulls

12. Fit As A Fiddle And Ready To Go!

Group V

1. Twins Riding An Escalator
(Enharmonic scales B Major and C Flat Major)

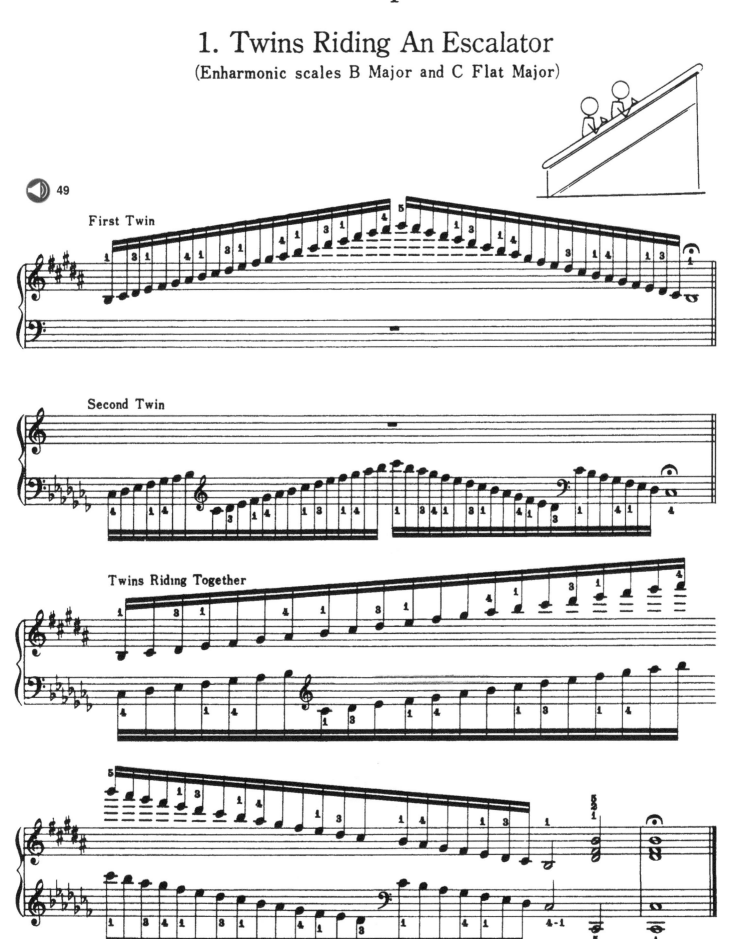

2. Twins Riding In A Glass Elevator

(Enharmonic scales F sharp Major and G flat Major)

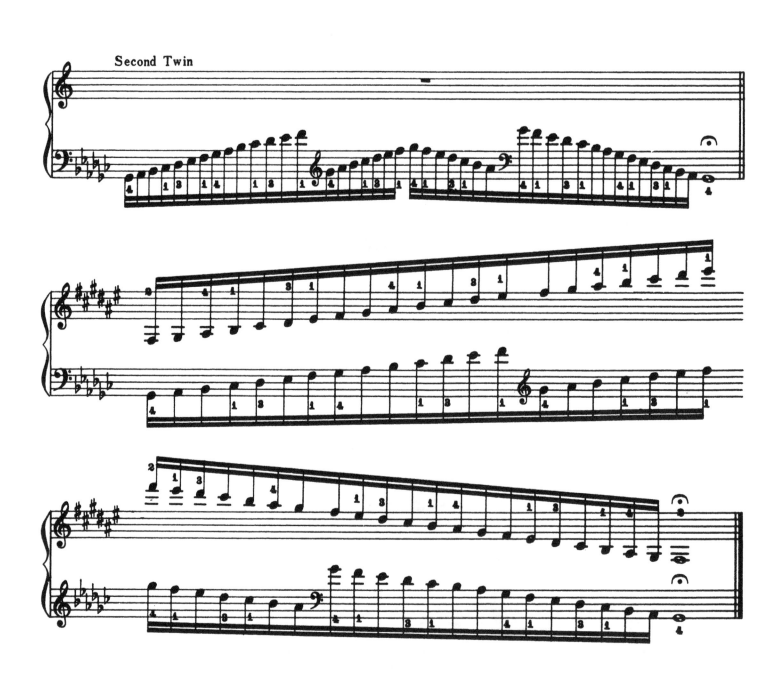

First Twin

Second Twin

3. Twins Riding In A Ski Lift

Enharmonic scales { C sharp Major
D flat Major

51 First Twin

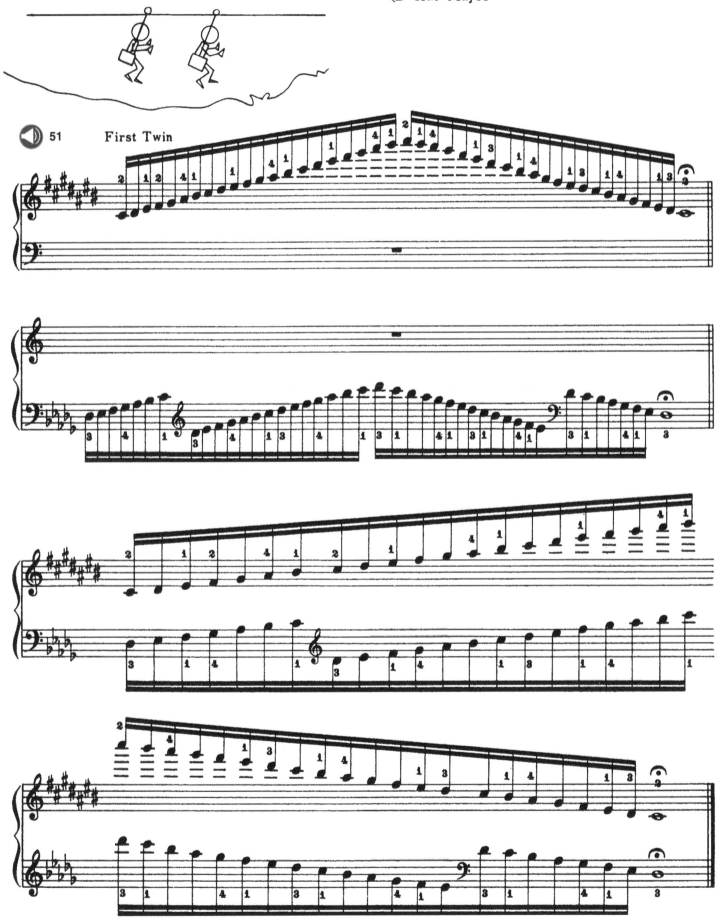

4. Riding A Tandem

(WITH THREE RELATIVES)

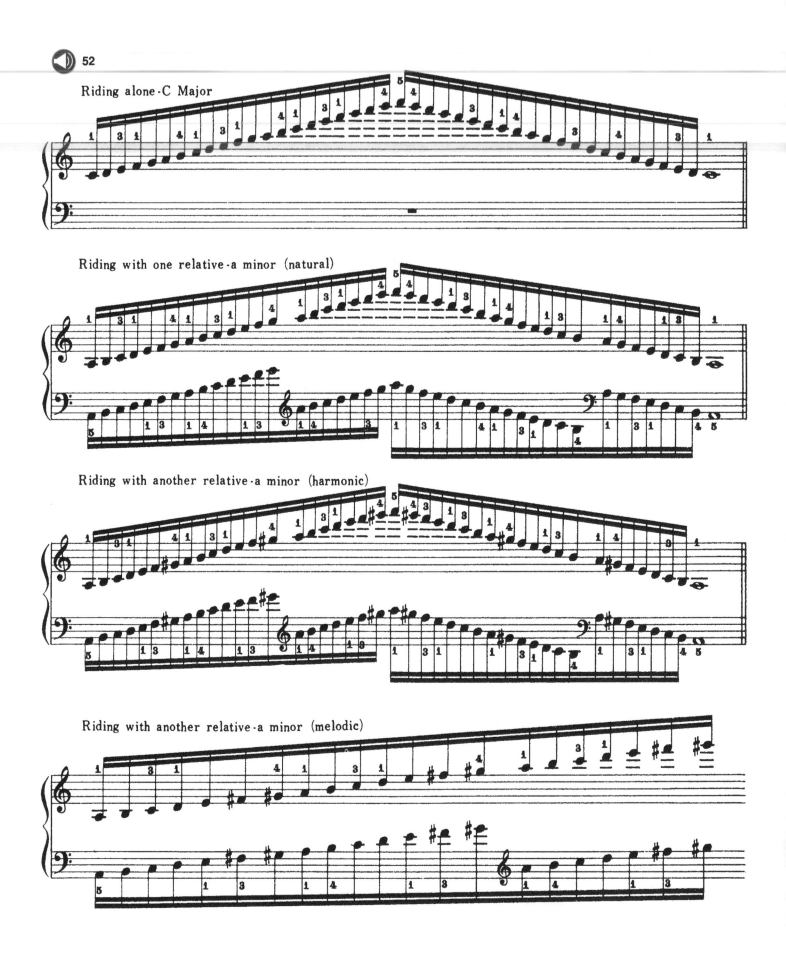

52

Riding alone · C Major

Riding with one relative · a minor (natural)

Riding with another relative · a minor (harmonic)

Riding with another relative · a minor (melodic)

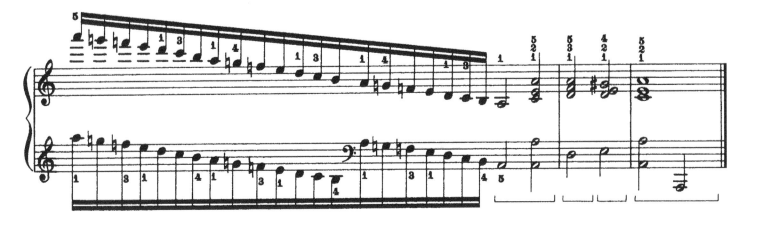

5. Badminton

No Key Signature
Bitonal

6. Sky Writing

7. Flying Saucer Ride

(Whole Tone Scale)

8. Caught On A Drawbridge!

 56

Drawbridge going up

Drawbridge going down

9. Riding A Kayak In The Rapids

(Changing meters)

10. On A Pogo Stick

(Tone Clusters)

11. Parachute Jumping

No Key Signature
No time signature
Pentatonic Scale
Tone clusters

59

12. Fit As A Fiddle And Ready To Go!

A DOZEN A DAY

by *Edna Mae Burnam*

The **A Dozen A Day** books are universally recognized as one of the most remarkable technique series on the market for all ages! Each book in this series contains short warm-up exercises to be played at the beginning of each practice session, providing excellent day-to-day training for the student. All book/audio versions include orchestrated accompaniments by Ric Ianonne.

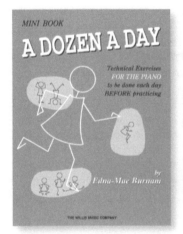

MINI BOOK
00404073 Book Only $5.99
00406472 Book/Audio $9.99

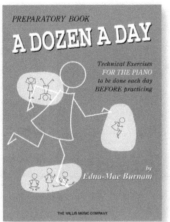

PREPARATORY BOOK
00414222 Book Only $5.99
00406476 Book/Audio $9.99

BOOK 1
00413366 Book Only $5.99
00406481 Book/Audio $9.99

BOOK 2
00413826 Book Only $5.99
00406485 Book/Audio $9.99

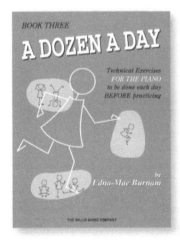

BOOK 3
00414136 Book Only $6.99
00416760 Book/Audio $10.99

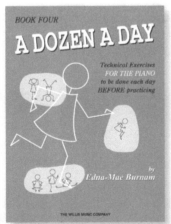

BOOK 4
00415686 Book Only $6.99
00416761 Book/Audio $10.99

**PLAY WITH EASE
IN MANY KEYS**
00416395 Book Only $5.99

**A DOZEN A DAY
ANTHOLOGY**
00158307 Book/Audio $24.99

WILLIS MUSIC

EXCLUSIVELY DISTRIBUTED BY

HAL•LEONARD®

Prices, contents, and availability subject to change without notice. Prices listed in U.S. funds.

CLASSIC PIANO REPERTOIRE

The *Classic Piano Repertoire* series includes popular as well as lesser-known pieces from a select group of composers out of the Willis piano archives. Every piece has been newly engraved and edited with the aim to preserve each composer's original intent and musical purpose.

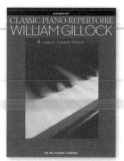

WILLIAM GILLOCK - ELEMENTARY

8 Great Piano Solos

Dance in Ancient Style • Little Flower Girl of Paris • On a Paris Boulevard • Rocking Chair Blues • Sliding in the Snow • Spooky Footsteps • A Stately Sarabande • Stormy Weather.

00416957 ....$8.99

WILLIAM GILLOCK - INTERMEDIATE TO ADVANCED

12 Exquisite Piano Solos

Classic Carnival • Etude in A Major (The Coral Sea) • Etude in E Minor • Etude in G Major (Toboggan Ride) • Festive Piece • A Memory of Vienna • Nocturne • Polynesian Nocturne • Sonatina in Classic Style • Sonatine • Sunset • Valse Etude.

00416912 .... $12.99

EDNA MAE BURNAM - ELEMENTARY

8 Great Piano Solos

The Clock That Stopped • The Friendly Spider • A Haunted House • New Shoes • The Ride of Paul Revere • The Singing Cello • The Singing Mermaid • Two Birds in a Tree.

00110228 ....$8.99

EDNA MAE BURNAM - INTERMEDIATE TO ADVANCED

13 Memorable Piano Solos

Butterfly Time • Echoes of Gypsies • Hawaiian Leis • Jubilee! • Longing for Scotland • Lovely Senorita • The Mighty Amazon River • Rumbling Rumba • The Singing Fountain • Song of the Prairie • Storm in the Night • Tempo Tarantelle • The White Cliffs of Dover.

00110229 .... $12.99

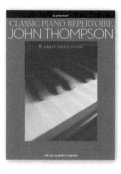

JOHN THOMPSON - ELEMENTARY

9 Great Piano Solos

Captain Kidd • Drowsy Moon • Dutch Dance • Forest Dawn • Humoresque • Southern Shuffle • Tiptoe • Toy Ships • Up in the Air.

00111968 ....$8.99

JOHN THOMPSON - INTERMEDIATE TO ADVANCED

12 Masterful Piano Solos

Andantino (from Concerto in D Minor) • The Coquette • The Faun • The Juggler • Lagoon • Lofty Peaks • Nocturne • Rhapsody Hongroise • Scherzando in G Major • Tango Carioca • Valse Burlesque • Valse Chromatique.

00111969 .... $12.99

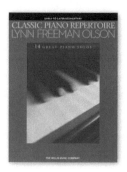

LYNN FREEMAN OLSON - EARLY TO LATER ELEMENTARY

14 Great Piano Solos

Caravan • Carillon • Come Out! Come Out! (Wherever You Are) • Halloween Dance • Johnny, Get Your Hair Cut! • Jumping the Hurdles • Monkey on a Stick • Peter the Pumpkin Eater • Pony Running Free • Silent Shadows • The Sunshine Song • Tall Pagoda • Tubas and Trumpets • Winter's Chocolatier.

00294722 ....$9.99

LYNN FREEMAN OLSON - EARLY TO MID-INTERMEDIATE

13 Distinctive Piano Solos

Band Wagon • Brazilian Holiday • Cloud Paintings • Fanfare • The Flying Ship • Heroic Event • In 1492 • Italian Street Singer • Mexican Serenade • Pageant Dance • Rather Blue • Theme and Variations • Whirlwind.

00294720 .... $9.99

WILLIS MUSIC

CLOSER LOOK View sample pages and hear audio excerpts online at www.halleonard.com

www.willispianomusic.com

 www.facebook.com/willispianomusic